OUR EARTH IN ACTION

SEAS AND COASTS

Chris Oxlade

W

FRANKLIN WATTS

This edition published in 2014 by Franklin Watts

Copyright © 2014 Franklin Watts

Franklin Watts
338 Euston Road
London NW1 3BH

Franklin Watts Australia
Level 17/207 Kent Street
Sydney, NSW 2000

A CIP catalogue record for this book is available
from the British Library.

Dewey number: 551.46

ISBN 978 1 4451 3197 9

Printed in China

Franklin Watts is a division of Hachette Children's Books,
an Hachette UK company.
www.hachette.co.uk

Artwork: John Alston
Editor: Sarah Ridley
Design: Thomas Keenes
Editor in Chief: John C. Miles
Art director: Jonathan Hair
Picture research: Diana Morris

Picture credits:
Roger Bamber/Alamy: 17. Blackbeck/istockphoto: 18. Rob Broek/istockphoto: 25b.
David Chadwick/istockphoto: 20-21. Amanda Cotton/istockphoto: 8-9.
Victor Lord Denovan/istockphoto: 21t. Digital Globe/Rex Features: 15t.
Erik Ellers/istockphoto: 6-7. Terry Fincher/Alamy: 29. Ann Taylor-Hughes/istockphoto: 5.
Zoltan Kovacs/istockphoto: 23t. Dr Ken Macdonald/SPL: 10. Roger Manns/Alamy: 24.
Xavier Marchant/Shutterstock: 19t. Louise Murray/Alamy: 27. NASA: 4t, 23b.
David Noton/Alamy: 28. Nicholas Pavlov/Getty Images: 11. Pelamis Wave Power Ltd: 25t.
Picturebank/Alamy: 22. Dan Rafla/Getty Images: 14-15. Stephen Rees/istockphoto: 13b.
Jeff Rotman/Alamy: 9t. Reto Steffen/istockphoto: 13t. Martin Strmko/istockphoto: 6t.
David Wall/Alamy: 16. Yegorius /Shutterstock: front cover. *Every attempt has been made to clear
copyright. Should there be any inadvertent omission please apply to the publisher
for rectification.*

CONTENTS

ABOUT SEAS AND COASTS

From our position on the Earth's surface it is hard to appreciate how our world is dominated by water. But from space, it's easy to see why the Earth is known as the 'blue planet', for two-thirds of the surface is covered with water. This fact makes the Earth a very special place.

SEAS AND OCEANS

The huge area of water on the Earth's surface is normally divided into five oceans — the Pacific Ocean, the Atlantic Ocean, the Indian Ocean, the Southern Ocean and the Arctic Ocean. In addition, there are areas of water called seas. The words 'sea' and 'ocean' are often used in place of each other. There is no rule to say what is an ocean and what is a sea, but in general an ocean is a vast, deep area of water thousands of kilometres across, whereas a sea is a smaller area of water partly enclosed by land (such as the Caribbean Sea or the Mediterranean Sea). The largest of

▲ This photo was taken from space. The oceans look blue because blue light from the Sun reflects off the water.

Arctic Ocean

Baltic Sea

North Sea

Black Sea

Caspian Sea

Atlantic Ocean

Pacific Ocean

Mediterranean Sea

South China Sea

Caribbean Sea

Pacific Ocean

Indian Ocean

Southern Ocean

◄ The world's oceans and major seas.

the world's inland lakes are also called seas. Overall, 97% of all the water on Earth is found in the oceans, and more than half of that is in the Pacific. The oceans are many kilometres deep, and the ocean floors are the least-explored parts of the planet. Here there are giant underwater volcanoes, deep trenches and vast flat plains.

COASTS

A coast is where the land meets and interacts with the sea. Coasts are dynamic places, where the landscape is constantly changed by the action of waves and currents. In some places the land is eroded away and in others it is built up, creating spectacular cliffs, bays, headlands, beaches and dunes. The world has a staggering 500,000 km of coastline — enough to stretch twelve times around the equator.

Where the water came from

When the Earth was formed, about 4,500 million years ago, there were no oceans. Water was mixed up in the molten rocky material of the Earth. Gradually gases such as water vapour, nitrogen and carbon dioxide came to the surface. When the water cooled it formed rain, and over hundreds of millions of years oceans were formed.

▼ *A jagged coastline, created by the sea breaking up rocks.*

IN THE OCEANS

Seawater is salty because substances called salts are dissolved in it. The most common salt in seawater is sodium chloride, but there are also salts that contain magnesium, calcium and potassium. On average, 1 kg of seawater contains about 25 g of dissolved salts. But seawater varies — for example, the Atlantic is saltier than the Pacific.

Life in the oceans

▲ Coral reefs grow in shallow, warm seas, and they teem with life.

The oceans are the Earth's largest environment for living things. The majority of marine animals and all marine plants live in the top 150 m of water, where light penetrates. At the bottom of the food chain there are countless billions of microscopic plants, called phytoplankton, and microscopic animals, called zooplankton. Some animals live deep down on the dark ocean floor. They feed on the remains of dead animals that drift down from above. On the coasts, plants and animals can survive, submerged, at high tide and in the air at low tide.

LIGHT, HEAT AND PRESSURE

Sunlight that shines into the sea is gradually absorbed as it goes down into the water. So as you move deeper into the water, there is less and less light, and eventually no light at all. Even in the clearest seawater, it is completely dark below a depth of 250 m. Heat from the Sun warms the water at the surface. But below a few hundred metres the water is always very cold, and deep down is close to freezing. Water makes a push on everything in it. This push is called water pressure, and it increases with depth. Hundreds of metres down, the pressure is so great that it would crush a diver.

▶ *A diagram of the water cycle. Water is constantly moving between the oceans, the atmosphere and the land. Water vapour in the atmosphere comes from evaporation of seawater and water in the soil. This falls to the surface when it turns into rain or snow (precipitation). Some flows back to the oceans along streams and rivers, and some re-evaporates into the air.*

ICE AND ICEBERGS

In the polar regions the seas are permanently frozen, forming sea ice. In winter the sea ice thickens, and its edges spread outwards; in summer it retreats again. The Arctic Ocean is permanently frozen around the North Pole, and around the Antarctic continent are areas of frozen sea called ice shelves. Icebergs are pieces of ice floating in the sea. They are broken sea ice or chunks of glacier that have fallen off into the sea.

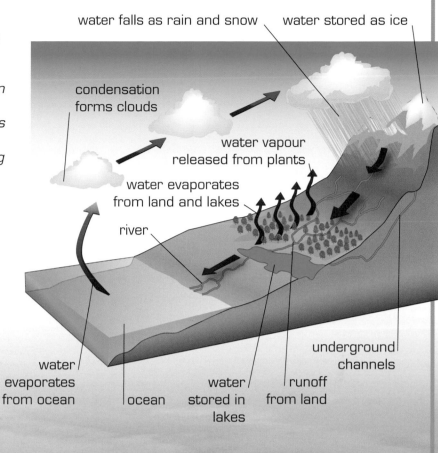

water falls as rain and snow   water stored as ice

condensation forms clouds

water vapour released from plants

water evaporates from land and lakes

river

water evaporates from ocean

ocean

water stored in lakes

runoff from land

underground channels

▼ *Icebergs are carried along by ocean currents. The largest take months to melt completely.*

7

THE SEA-BED

The average depth of the world's seas and oceans is 3,500 m. However, around the edges of the continents, the average depth is just 130 m. This area is called the continental shelf. In some places the shelf is hundreds of kilometres wide, but in others it is just a few kilometres wide. The majority of marine life lives on the continental shelf. At the edge of the shelf the sea-bed slopes down, to an average depth of 4,000 m.

THE CONTINENTAL SLOPE

The continental slope leads from the continental shelf to the ocean floor below. In many places sediment from large rivers covers the continental shelf and the continental slope. Avalanches of sediment called turbidity currents flow down the slope, set off by earthquakes

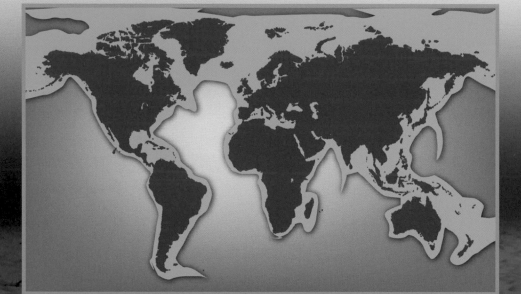

◄ A map of most of the world's continental shelves, excluding Antarctica (shelves are shown in blue along the coasts of the continents).

and storms. They erode deep canyons in the slope, and leave deposits of sediment called deep-sea fans on the ocean floor below.

THE ABYSSAL PLAINS

Out in the oceans the ocean floor is generally flat, but there are ridges and rises, and deep trenches (see page 10). Covering about half the ocean floor are vast, flat areas called abyssal plains. They lie between 4,000 and 6,000 m below the surface of the ocean.

SEA-BED SEDIMENTS

The sea-bed is covered with layers of sediment. Close to the continents the sediments are made from rocky particles formed by erosion of the land. In mid-ocean, the sediments are the remains of marine animals and plants that drift down from above. These sediments are called oozes. Some areas of the Pacific Ocean floor are covered with small lumps called manganese nodules, formed from chemicals in the water. These grow by just 1 mm in a million years!

Discovering the ocean floor

The darkness and enormous pressure makes the ocean floor a difficult place to explore. Specialised craft called submersibles are needed to reach here. A few are manned, but most are remotely operated vehicles (ROVs). They take video and photographs and gather samples of water and sediments. The shape of the ocean floor is measured with sonar, carried by ROVs and by surface ships.

▼ *Scientists in a submersible explore the ocean floor.*

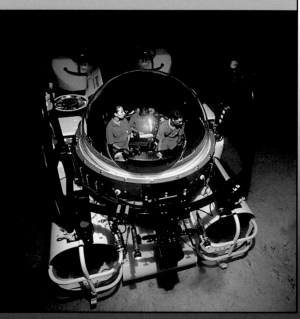

◄ *The sea-bed of a shallow sea. The ripples in the sediment are caused by currents.*

MOUNTAINS AND TRENCHES

The ocean floor is littered with mountainous features called ridges, seamounts and trenches. The position of these features is linked closely to the tectonic plates that make up the Earth's crust. Most are situated along the edges of the plates (the plate boundaries).

SPREADING RIDGES

A place where two tectonic plates are spreading apart is called a constructive boundary. As the plates move apart, magma (molten rock) rises from under the crust and solidifies to form new rock. This process is very slow (the plates move at just a few centimetres a year) but creates a mountainous ridge on the ocean floor thousands of metres high. One example is the Mid-Atlantic Ridge, which stretches for 11,300 km.

TRENCHES

Ocean trenches are vast furrows in the ocean floor. They can be thousands of kilometres long, hundreds of kilometres wide and thousands of metres deep. They form at places called subduction zones, where one tectonic plate dips down under another, pulling the ocean floor with it. Most ocean trenches are around the Pacific rim. The Mariana Trench, south of Japan, includes the deepest point of all, the Challenger Deep, 10,950 m below sea level. The water pressure in the deepest parts of the ocean is immense. In the Challenger Deep, for example, the pressure would feel the same as a tonne weight pressing on every square centimetre of your body.

VOLCANOES AND SEAMOUNTS

Reaching up from the ocean floor are thousands of undersea volcanoes. Where these grow tall enough they break the surface,

Black smokers

'Black smoker' is another name for a hydrothermal vent. Here, hot water, made dark by minerals including sulphur, gushes from the sea-bed. Hydrothermal vents are found along spreading ridges, where there are hot volcanic rocks. The water can be as hot as 350°C, but high pressure stops it boiling. Bacteria use the sulphur as a source of energy and, in turn, are a source of food for peculiar animals, including giant worms and sightless crabs.

making islands. The Hawaiian Islands are a chain of islands formed as the Pacific tectonic plate has moved slowly over a 'hot spot' in the crust, where magma wells up from underneath. Volcanic mountains under the water are called seamounts.

▶ *The Hawaiian Islands were formed as the crust moved over a hot spot, as shown here.*

▼ *This island in the Hawaiian chain is a remnant of an old volcano.*

extinct volcano

extinct volcano

extinct volcano

active volcano

Pacific Ocean

movement of Earth's crust

hot spot

magma

TIDES AND CURRENTS

The water in the oceans is never still. Tides make the surface rise and fall and make water flow around coasts and in and out of bays and estuaries.

Winds and heating by the Sun create a complex pattern of ocean currents that carry warm and cool water around the globe.

SURFACE CURRENTS

Surface currents are driven by prevailing winds (a prevailing wind is a wind from a particular direction that blows most of the time at a certain place). Surface currents can be hundreds of kilometres wide and flow at speeds up to 220 km per day. Examples of currents are the Gulf Stream and North Atlantic Drift, which carry warm water from the tropics along the east coast of North America and into the North Atlantic. The Humboldt (or Peru) Current carries cold water from the Antarctic up the west coast of South America.

DEEP CURRENTS

Currents also flow deep down in the ocean. They are caused by differences in water temperature and salinity (the amount of salt dissolved in the water). For example, water in the Arctic cools and so becomes more dense. It sinks and flows across the ocean floor. Deep currents flow at just a few metres per day — much slower than surface currents.

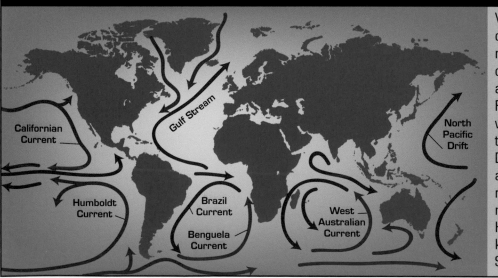

Currents and climate

Californian Current

Gulf Stream

North Pacific Drift

Humboldt Current

Brazil Current

Benguela Current

West Australian Current

Warm and cold currents have a major effect on the climate of large areas of the world. For example, the warm waters of the North Atlantic Drift keep winters around the coasts of northern Europe mild. The cool Humboldt Current keeps the coast of South America dry.

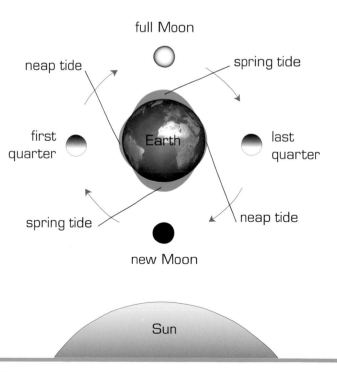

◀ *These two photographs show the same location at high tide and low tide, which happen just six hours apart.*

TIDES

The gravitational pull of the Moon and Sun pulls on the water in the oceans, making it bulge upwards slightly. As the Earth spins, the bulges move across the oceans, creating rises and falls in sea level called tides. Most places have two high tides and two low tides a day. Tidal range is the difference in height between high tide and low tide. It is largest during spring tides, when the Moon and Sun pull in the same direction, and smallest during neap tides, when the Moon and Sun are pulling at right angles to each other.

▶ *The gravity of the Moon creates a bulge in the oceans on both sides of the planet. Spring tides happen when the Sun's gravity is in line with the Moon's.*

WAVES

Wind blowing across the surface of the sea causes waves. The stronger the wind, the larger the waves become. The wind's energy is stored in the waves. Although waves move across the sea's surface, the water itself does not move along. Instead, the particles in the water move in circles. This is why floating objects bob up and down as waves pass.

WAVE FORMATION

The size of waves depends on the strength of the wind and the distance of open water that the wind blows across. The distance is called the fetch. Waves begin as ripples, but if the wind keeps blowing, they gain more energy and grow as they travel. Gale-force winds blowing across hundreds of kilometres of ocean create huge waves, the biggest more than 30 m high from trough to crest. Large waves can travel for hundreds of kilometres before they die down, producing a swell even where conditions are calm.

▼ *In gale-force winds the tops of waves are ripped off, creating broken seas like this.*

BREAKING WAVES

As waves move into shallow coastal water they slow down and become higher and closer together. The tops of the waves overtake the bases, and the waves topple and break. On beaches the breaking waves move up the beach and then flow back down again. These movements are called swash and backwash.

TSUNAMIS

A tsunami is a wave set off by an undersea earthquake, landslide or explosive volcanic eruption. In the case of an earthquake, the ocean floor moves up or down suddenly, disturbing the surface above. At first a tsunami wave may be less than a metre high, but the distance from its crest to its trough can be hundreds of metres, and it can travel at hundreds of kilometres per hour. When it reaches shallow water at a coast, a tsunami wave breaks like any other wave, but may grow to 30 m high and sweep far inland, causing catastrophic damage.

▲ Satellite images of the city of Banda Aceh, Indonesia, before and after the 2004 Asian tsunami.

Mega tsunamis

The most destructive tsunami of recent times was the Asian tsunami of 2004, which killed around a quarter of a million people. But there is evidence of much larger tsunamis in the past. And scientists think that one day a giant landslide may occur from a volcano on the island of La Palma in the Canary Islands, creating tsunamis on the coasts of North and South America on the other side of the Atlantic.

COASTAL EROSION

Where waves hit coasts they cause erosion — they break down the rocks of the coast. The eroded material is carried away by waves and currents. Erosion creates coastal features such as bays and headlands, and eroded material builds up to form beaches (see pages 20-21).

WATER POWER

Waves erode the coast in several ways. Breaking waves produce enormous forces that pull rocks apart. When waves break against rocks, trapped air is forced into cracks, weakening the rock. Waves also smash loose pieces of material into rocks. The erosion cuts away at the base of cliffs, undermining them. The rate of erosion depends on the rock itself (hard rock erodes more slowly than soft rock), and on the power of the waves. Waves also smash and grind pieces of rock together, breaking them up and making them smooth. This process forms pebbles from bits of rock.

BAYS AND HEADLANDS

Where there are areas of softer rocks and harder rocks along a coast, the soft rocks are eroded more quickly, and the coast curves inland, forming bays with beaches. The harder rocks are left extending into the sea, forming rocky headlands, which often erode into other features (see page 18). In some places, the sea breaks through a narrow band of hard rock and erodes a bay behind.

◄ *A headland formed where hard rocks have been eroded more slowly than in the bay beyond.*

▲ *Coasts made of soft rocks such as clay erode quickly. Landslides are common as the base of the cliffs is eaten away.*

EROSION PROBLEMS

Coastal erosion is a problem where there are buildings on coasts made from soft rocks. Erosion undermines foundations until the buildings collapse into the sea. The coast can be eroded at the rate of many metres per year, so that buildings originally hundreds of metres inland are eventually destroyed.

Erosion protection

Coasts are often protected from erosion by structures called coastal defences. Defences include concrete walls and huge concrete blocks that soak up the energy in waves, protecting the soft rocks behind. Defences are vital to protect coastal towns and cities. But there is a debate about whether rural coastlines should be protected or left to erode naturally, as protection is expensive and sometimes fails to do its job.

COASTAL FEATURES

Waves erode the coastline into various features. Cliffs are formed where erosion wears away land that stands well above sea level. The sea erodes the base of the cliff, and if the rock is soft, the cliff face collapses. The most dramatic features are formed where headlands are eroded, leaving caves, arches and towering rock stacks.

CAVES AND ARCHES

Waves that arrive at a headland tend to bend round and hit its sides. Where there are cracks in the rock, the waves slowly erode the sides of the cracks, making them wider. Eventually cracks develop into caves. If erosion continues, a cave gets deeper and deeper, and may break through to the other side of the headland, forming a tunnel. The part of the headland over the tunnel is called an arch.

STACKS AND STUMPS

The sides of a tunnel under an arch are gradually eroded, making the tunnel wider. Eventually the arch becomes too long to support its own weight, and it collapses into the sea. This leaves a pillar of rock called a stack out to sea at the end of the headland. Stacks can be hundreds of metres high. The base of a stack slowly erodes away and eventually the stack collapses into the sea, leaving a rocky stump. The whole process of cave, arch, stack and stump formation is repeated many times as a headland is eroded away.

▼ *This natural arch is at Durdle Door in southern Britain.*

Coral reefs

A coral reef is a rocky barrier in shallow water, normally within a few hundred metres of a coast. The rock is made of the skeletons of billions of tiny marine animals called polyps. Reefs make waves break offshore, leaving an area of calm sea between the reef and the shore. The Great Barrier Reef on the east coast of Australia is 2,028 km long and is the largest feature on Earth made by animals. Coral atolls are rings of coral islands around a central lagoon. They form around volcanic islands, and are left behind when the volcanoes become extinct and then sink slowly back into the sea.

▼ *Waves breaking on a coral reef.*

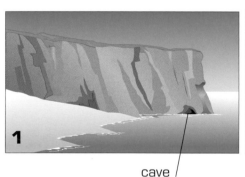

1

cave

2

arch

3

stack

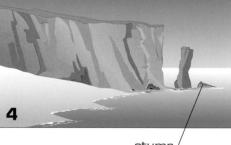

4

stump

◀ *The stages in the erosion of a headland. The process shown here may take thousands of years.*

BEACHES

A beach is made up of billions of particles of material, which can be tiny bits of rock, small or large pebbles, or fragments of the shells of marine animals. Not all beaches are yellow and sandy — some are made of black volcanic sand and others entirely of pebbles.

BEACH FORMATION

Beaches are made up of material dumped on the coast by the action of waves and currents. The rocky material comes from the erosion of coastal rocks and from sediments washed down rivers to the sea. It is often carried along the coast from other areas before being deposited. Beaches tend to have bands of different materials along them because the material is sorted as waves push it up and down the beach. Beaches are always changing shape because their material is eroded and deposited again during storms.

MOVING SAND

Waves rarely hit a beach head on — they normally hit at an angle. The wave sweeps up the beach, pushing beach material up and along the beach. Then the water runs straight back down to the sea, carrying the material with it. The material is deposited slightly further along the

▼ Sand dunes create a natural barrier between the beach and the land behind.

beach than before. This movement of material is called longshore drift. It often carries material away from beaches, leaving them smaller than before. Some tourist beaches are protected from longshore drift by wooden barriers called groynes.

▲ Groynes prevent sand from moving along a beach.

SAND DUNES

Sand dunes form where dry sand is blown up a beach and out of the reach of high tides. Plants grow in the sand and their roots make it stable. Then the dunes grow as more sand is blown onto them.

Raised beaches

On some coasts there are flat areas of land a few metres above where the sea reaches, with higher land behind. These flat areas are old beaches called raised beaches. Since they were formed, the land has lifted upwards, leaving them high and dry. Land rises up for many reasons. One is that the weight of ice that pressed the land down during the last ice age has been removed, allowing the land to lift up again.

ESTUARIES AND DELTAS

Some coastal features are formed where rivers flowing from inland arrive at the coast. An estuary is a place at a river mouth where the coast curves far inland. A delta is an area of low-lying coastal land formed from sediments carried in river water and washed out to sea.

MIXING WATER

In an estuary, fresh water from a river and salt water from the sea mix together. The bed of the estuary is made up of sandy and muddy sediment from the river. At low tide the bed is revealed. River water enters the top of the estuary and flows through channels in to the sea at the bottom. At high tide the estuary is filled with seawater, and the sea-bed is covered. The edges of estuaries are often lined with salt marshes that are only flooded during spring tides (see page 13).

▲ *An estuary at low tide. The silt has been deposited by the river.*

BARS AND SPITS

A sand bar is a barrier of sediment out in the sea. Bars form where the coast bends sharply inland, such as at an estuary. Longshore drift carries the material past the bend, forming the barrier. A spit is a hook-shaped area of beach at the end of a sand bar. The area behind a spit in often filled with sediment, forming a salt marsh.

DELTAS

When a river flows into the sea, its water slows down and the sediment that it has carried downstream is deposited on the sea-bed. At the end of large rivers that carry a vast amount of sediment, the sediment builds up into new land called a delta that sticks out into the sea. The river flows across the delta to the sea. Some deltas, such as the Nile delta and the Ganges delta, are hundreds of kilometres across.

▼ *A satellite photograph of the Nile delta in Egypt. The silt from the river makes this fertile farming land.*

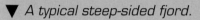

Fjords and rias

A fjord is a deep, narrow inlet into a coast that is many kilometres long. Fjords are valleys that were gouged out by glaciers thousands of years ago during the ice ages. When the ice sheets retreated, the sea flooded the valleys. A ria is similar, but is a river valley flooded by a rise in sea level.

▼ *A typical steep-sided fjord.*

SEA AND COAST RESOURCES

The Earth's seas and coasts are important resources for us. The seas provide us with food and raw materials such as oil, are a vital transport route, and are a source of renewable energy. The coasts supply us with food and in many places are venues for tourism and leisure pursuits, such as swimming, sailing and other water sports.

FISHING

Each year we catch tens of millions of tonnes of fish and other marine animals for food. The catches come from surface waters (such as tuna and mackerel), the sea-bed (such as cod and crabs) and the coast (such as shellfish). Fishing takes place on a small scale, with individual fishermen working on coasts, and on an industrial scale, with fleets of large boats working far offshore.

▼ *Fishing continues to be an important job for many people around the world.*

Salt and water

Both salt and water are extracted from the sea. Salt is extracted by putting seawater in shallow pools and allowing the water to evaporate, leaving the salt. Water is extracted in coastal areas where there is no source of fresh water. The salty water is 'desalinated' by allowing it to evaporate into water vapour, which leaves the salt behind, and then condensing the vapour back to water and collecting it.

FOSSIL FUELS

Oil and gas are often found in rocks under the sea-bed. They are formed from the remains of sea creatures that lived millions of years ago. The oil and gas are trapped in rock layers, often many kilometres under the sea-bed. They are extracted by production platforms that stand on the sea-bed on long legs.

ENERGY FROM THE OCEANS

There is energy in moving water and in waves. There are a few tidal power stations around the world. At a tidal power station, water is trapped as the tide rises and falls, and allowed to flow through turbines, which turn electricity generators. Engineers are testing various designs of turbines that capture the energy in ocean currents. Experimental wave-energy power stations are also being tested.

▼ *A wave-energy generator bends as waves pass by, creating electricity.*

SEA TRANSPORT

Ships can carry vast amounts of goods or materials very efficiently, and can reach hundreds of ports around the world. There are tens of thousands of ships travelling the world's oceans, specialised to carry bulk materials such as grain or oil, or mixed goods in metal containers.

▶ *Container ships operate from vast container ports.*

CASE STUDY: THE PACIFIC

The Pacific Ocean is by far the world's biggest ocean. It covers a third of the Earth's surface, is twice as large as the Atlantic, and has more water surface area than the world's entire land area. It stretches from the Arctic to the Antarctic, and from Asia to the Americas.

OCEAN FLOOR FEATURES

The Pacific Ocean is surrounded by subduction zones, so there are many ocean trenches around its edges. They include the Mariana Trench, the world's deepest, and the Aleutian Trench, the world's longest. There is also a vast spreading ridge — the East Pacific Rise. The floor of the Pacific is littered with thousands of submerged seamounts. There are also about 25,000 volcanic islands in the Pacific, most surrounded by coral reefs.

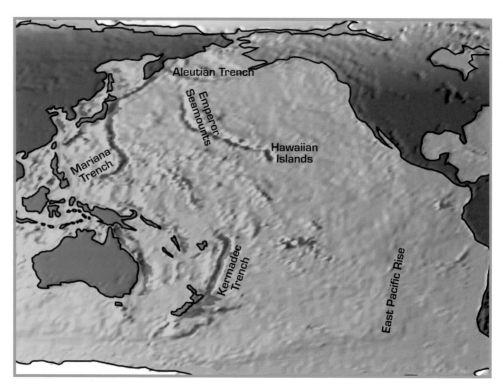

Aleutian Trench

Emperor Seamounts

Mariana Trench

Hawaiian Islands

Kermadec Trench

East Pacific Rise

▲ *The floor of the Pacific is covered with amazing features.*

TSUNAMIS AND TYPHOONS

Earthquakes are frequent around the edge of the Pacific because of the movement of tectonic plates at subduction zones. This makes the Pacific prone to tsunamis, and these can travel right across the Pacific. In 1960, a tsunami set off by an earthquake in Peru struck Japan.

Typhoon is the name for a tropical cyclone in the western Pacific. Typhoons begin as clusters of storms in the tropics. The storms begin to spin and move across the ocean, feeding on heat from the warm waters. Typhoons can grow up to 500 km across and contain winds as strong as 170 km per hour. Typhoons cause extensive damage to the Pacific coasts of Asia during the typhoon season (May to December).

▶ *A coral island in the Pacific Ocean, surrounded by its own reef.*

Pacific ocean facts

Area: 155,557,000 km²
Maximum width: 17,700 km
Average depth: 4,200 m
Deepest point: Challenger Deep, 10,950 m
Length of coastline: 135,663 km

El Niño

El Niño (say *el nee-neo*) is a weather event in the Pacific. In most years, ocean currents bring cold water to the coast of Peru between June and December, and warm water for the rest of the year. But in some years westerly winds are too weak to carry the warm water away. This affects the normal weather patterns in North America and the countries of the eastern Pacific, causing floods and droughts.

ENVIRONMENTAL ISSUES

Like most natural environments on our planet, the seas and coasts have been affected by our activities. The most obvious problem is pollution of the water by all sorts of waste materials, from plastic bottles to sewage. Other problems include over-fishing and rising sea levels.

POLLUTION AT SEA

Unfortunately, the sea is a convenient dumping ground for waste from the land and from ships. Solid waste such as plastic bottles, wooden palettes, oil drums and old fishing nets are often washed up on shore. But other sorts of waste are not so obvious. In many places sewage, sometimes untreated, still flows straight into the sea. This is unpleasant and potentially dangerous to swimmers and surfers. Industrial waste, pesticides and fertilisers are all washed down rivers into the sea. Some waste chemicals build up in the bodies of marine animals, such as shellfish, and are then passed up the food chain.

OIL SPILLS

Accidental spills of crude oil from oil tankers are a particular problem. The oil spreads out to form an oil slick. If a slick reaches the coast the oil coats beaches and rocks, and kills sea birds and other animals. One of the world's most damaging oil spills happened in 1989, when the tanker *Exxon Valdez* went aground in Alaska. A much bigger oil spill occurred when an explosion on the *Deepwater Horizon* oil rig in 2010 led to 4.9 million barrels of crude oil spilling into the Gulf of Mexico. Experts are still counting the cost.

▲ *Outflow pipes carry sewage from treatment plants down to the sea, where the treated sewage flows into the water.*

RISING SEA LEVELS

Experts from the United Nation's Intergovernmental Panel on Climate Change estimate that sea levels around the world could rise by up to a metre by the year 2100. Sea levels are rising as ice caps (especially in Greenland) are slowly melting and seawater is slowly expanding due to global warming. Low-lying coastal regions, such as southern Bangladesh, and coral islands, such as the Maldives, will be at greater risk of flooding if we cannot slow global warming.

LOOKING AFTER SEAS AND COASTS

As well as being the habitat of a staggering variety of animals and plants, the seas and coasts are vitally important to us. They provide us with food and energy, and they have a huge impact on our climate. So we must take as much care of the seas and coasts as we do the land.

▼ *Cleaning up after the* Exxon Valdez *oil spill in 1989. The oil killed thousands of seabirds, seals and otters as well as millions of fish.*

GLOSSARY

active volcano a volcano that is erupting or has erupted in the last 10,000 years or so

constructive plate boundary a line along which two tectonic plates are moving apart

continental plate part of a tectonic plate under a continent, which is much thicker than an ocean plate

coral reef a rocky barrier in warm, shallow seas, made from the skeletons of sea creatures

crust the rocky top layer of the Earth

dune a hill made from sand

erosion the wearing away of the landscape

eruption the emission of lava, ash or gas from a volcano

estuary an inlet in the coast where a river flows into the sea

evaporation the change of state from liquid to gas

extinct volcano a volcano that is no longer active

foundations part of a building that are underground, supporting the weight of the rest of the building above

glacier a slow-moving river of ice

global warming the gradual warming of the Earth's atmosphere

headland a place where a strip of rock sticks out into the sea from the coast

hot spot a place far from any tectonic plate boundary where magma forces its way to the surface

ice age a period of time in the past when the climate was colder than today and thick ice sheets covered much of the northern hemisphere

ice cap a very thick (many kilometres in some places) sheet of ice covering some cold parts of the Earth

lava the name given to the molten, rocky part of magma when it comes out of a volcano

magma molten rock underground

mantle the thick layer of rock inside the Earth under the crust

marine to do with the sea

microscopic describes something that is too small to see with the naked eye (i.e. without a microscope)

ocean a vast, deep area of water on the Earth's surface

ocean plate part of a tectonic plate under the ocean, which is much thinner than a continental plate

plate boundary the line along which two tectonic plates meet

renewable energy energy that comes from renewable sources that will never run out, such as solar, wind and tidal energy

sea an area of water smaller than an ocean and normally partly surrounded by land

seamount a volcano that grows up from the ocean floor

sediment material made from millions of small particles of rock or other hard material

spreading ridge a raised line of rocks on the ocean floor, made where two tectonic plates are moving apart

tectonic plate one of the huge pieces that the Earth's crust is cracked into

trench a deep furrow in the ocean floor

tropics the region of the Earth's surface around the equator, between the tropics of Cancer and Capricorn

volcano a place where magma emerges onto the Earth's surface from under the crust

water vapour water in its gas form, which is always present in the air

Further information

BBC Science and Nature Oceans
A collection of short films relating to oceans.
www.bbc.co.uk/science/earth/water_and_ice/ocean

Office of Naval Research
The research branch of the US Navy. Excellent website covering various aspects of the seas and coasts.
www.onr.navy.mil/focus/ocean

Great Barrier Reef
The Australian Government's website about the Great Barrier Reef.
www.australia.gov.au/about-australia/australian-story/great-barrier-reef

National Oceanic and Atmospheric Administration
This US organisation carries out research into the oceans and the weather. They have a special website about ocean exploration.
www.noaa.gov/ocean.html

Ocean energy
News and information about the latest wave-power technology.
www.alternative-energy-news.info/technology/hydro/wave-power/

Paul H Yancey
Website of a biology professor at Whitman College, Washington, USA.
A complicated site, but lots of fantastic images and links about the deep sea and ocean floor.
http://people.whitman.edu/~yancey/deepsea.html

INDEX